# Figure in the Landscape

Also by Danny Gardner and published by Ginninderra Press
*Before I Press the Trigger*
*Brains In My Feet*

Danny Gardner

# Figure in the Landscape

# Acknowledgements

Previously published/performed:
'Ballerina' in *Hope in Progress* (Taurus Books, 1980)
'Carnarvon Gorge', 'In Wake of Adam Cullen' and 'Shopwindow Dummies' in *Poetsconsortium*, Poets at Petersham Bowlo
'End of Form' in *New Departures*, UK, No. 15 (1983), Third International Poetry Olympics edition
'Fraud of Reason' in *Chinese-Australian Literary Quarterly*
'From Arles, Provence' – performed by the Live Poets Players at Don Bank, 2017
'It Always Gets Me' – in *War to End All Wars,* 2018
'Love's Analergy' – in *Five Bells*, Poets Union monthly magazine
'Only the Men Are Dead' – in *100 Years of Anzac*
'The River' in *Litmus Suite* (Live Poets' Press, 1991)
'Sex' in *Five Live* (Live Poets' Press, 1994)
'Smiley (2)' – in *Poetry at the Pub*, Newcastle
'Space – Are You?' – performed at Sydney Writers Festival 2009 and published in *Mosaic*, Auburn Poets & Writers' Group Anthology, 2015
'Stare' – performed at Sydney Writers Festival 2010 and published in *Mosaic*, Auburn Poets and Writers' Group Anthology, 2015
'State of Disunion' – in *We've Got 30 Years* (Live Poets Press, 2020)
'Time Belongim You, Massa' – in *Mountain Secrets* (Ginninderra Press, 2019)

*Figure in the Landscape*
ISBN 978 1 76109 294 7
Copyright © text Danny Gardner 2022
Cover image: Alex Azabache from Pexels

First published 2022 by
**GINNINDERRA PRESS**
PO Box 3461 Port Adelaide 5015
www.ginninderrapress.com.au

# Contents

| | |
|---|---|
| Frontispiece | 9 |
| **Part One** | |
| Womerah Lane | 13 |
| Arthur Chidley | 14 |
| Federation Train | 15 |
| Plane-view | 17 |
| Derwent Water (Cumbria) | 18 |
| A Day Late | 19 |
| Nativity (Bethlehem, 1994) | 20 |
| Regarding Cezanne | 21 |
| Jonestown | 23 |
| A Clear Night in Memphis (Alexander's Destination) | 25 |
| Goya's Blind Guitarist | 27 |
| After Mabo | 28 |
| Night on Mount Ann | 30 |
| Ballerina | 31 |
| Smiley 2 | 32 |
| Thameside Cohorts (early 1980s) | 34 |
| Eyes of the Castaway | 55 |
| Liar-byrd | 58 |
| The Railway System (Another View) | 61 |
| Love's Analergy | 63 |
| **Part Two** | |
| Meeting Point | 67 |
| From the navigator of the Enola Gay | 69 |
| Fraud of Reason | 70 |
| Space – Are You? | 71 |
| Stare | 72 |
| At Burke's Grave | 74 |

| | |
|---|---|
| Spain, Are You Here? (early 1980s) | 76 |
| Only the Men Are Dead | 87 |
| Season's End | 89 |
| The Face | 91 |
| New Eye Age | 93 |
| MH 017 | 95 |
| Loose Tie | 96 |
| Ghost Bird | 98 |
| Carnarvon Gorge | 99 |
| In Harm's Way | 100 |
| To Ted Hughes | 101 |
| Chet Baker | 103 |
| Zeroes | 105 |
| How That Fellah Othello Got the Rap | 106 |
| Posterity Got it Wrong | 108 |
| It Always Gets Me | 109 |

Part Three

| | |
|---|---|
| In Wake of Adam Cullen | 113 |
| Shop Window Dummies | 115 |
| No Refuge | 117 |
| Old Poet | 118 |
| From Arles, Provence | 119 |
| AMSL | 131 |
| Tarangere, Tanzania | 133 |
| Grasping the Bacon | 134 |
| What Happened Last Night? | 136 |
| Inalarga Pass | 138 |
| Drought and Beyond | 139 |
| Moses at Finke | 141 |
| Birthnight | 142 |
| Time Belongim You, Massa | 143 |

| | |
|---|---:|
| Visiting Santa | 144 |
| 'All That is Left' | 146 |
| Flame-lighter | 148 |
| State of Disunion | 149 |
| Watching Men Moon Walk | 150 |
| Zoo Motions | 151 |

'Art is not what you see – but what you help others see.'
– Edgar Degas (1834–1917)

'The writing of a poem is a process of exploration.'
– Bruce Dawe (1930–2020)

# Frontispiece

'There is not much different to see each day
Not when you are this far in
The same bush clump each way you look
The same soil beneath your feet
In this place the sea once caressed
The sky to stare at you – the light to adorn you…
But no…everything looks the same from up there
No matter how you froth and glory down here – inside'

# Part One

# Womerah Lane

Looking up
at the lighted window
in a Womerah Lane boarding house
when street light was like moonlight,
when it was warm in July,
where I smiled in the mirror at the mayhem,
where my future beckoned
beyond the gas ring and the single bed, the open razor
the suitcase of memory.
I looked out that same window
to the blackness
where windmills once whirred
in the grain of first growing,
and could not yet
credit  that artist
taking his ease
at the picture he was forming…
The camera of his eye
on time delay
trying to be neutral and anonymous
like the motivation of my plays sent to Nimrod,
my romance stories to Cleo,
my 'green diary' that tried to become a novel
forty years ago…
Like the person burning that light now on Womerah Lane
that relatives back home would never recognise.

# Arthur Chidley

Public speaker in early 1900s Sydney – later interned at Callan Park Mental Hospital

Each day I come here to the Domain – it's like starting again.
Each day I come here, holding the book, the Answer –
as the malady grows ever urgent.
But, I am told, 'You can't talk about these things.'
The cancerous ghost that eats away at our relations,
that robs our Misses of their due station.
Each day the authorities wait for me to utter that fateful word,
each shadow that swallows this sward – fudges the line.
It is as though I am a religion only I can see.
Those eyes tell me, 'You're wrong!'
And each face carries home again
the dagger of habit:
but I tell you, I tell you – again and again,
how we have sex makes the world a misery!
Man's penetration of the woman's vagina injures them!
We must meet each other on equal ground:
woman's well-being must come first!

The brutish shun me.
The authorities arrest me
for wearing a toga and uttering that word: 'Coition'!
One more time in the twilight's prime.
But next Sunday I will be here again
just like the first time.
Holding the book,
the Answer!

## Federation Train

From well-meaning proclamations
the notion formed a contagion of unity.
But it was mostly spread by politicians and business types,
those who had the leisure
to think about prestige in foreign lands;
agitators stirred by the brethren of European example,
seekers of grace from the Buckingham Palace bosom.

To others, it was an idea before its time.
Cynics considered it all the talk of dreamers,
of white hands divorced from the common weal.
Those ready to plot their own class ascension
in defiance of the heat, flood and silence of reality.

For the romantics, fortified by poets' ballads,
it embodied an essential, spiritual intent,
plucking unerringly, if intermittently,
at the wanton fibre of some national soul.
It asked ordinary folk to inspire the mundane,
to step out onto an invisible limb;
to steal along country tracks by moonlight
where nuggets of opportunity once gleamed,
where bushrangers were still living legends,
where ancient spirits suffered scarce diminution
their Other-world catastrophe, carried in virtual secret.

In a climax to the Seers' wildest fantasies
of war obligations abroad, of pestilence at its door,
the Train moved beyond political chicanery
oblivious to Reconciliations it could not recognise
as necessary – sweeping up, too, those in ignorance or denial,
consuming the locally, regionally important
despite all its platitudes of inclusion –
like a bushfire, ignited.

# Plane-view

I begin to look down…
Clouds are heaped, cotton-wool balls;
their pressure released in rain lines over ocean.
Now giant snow monsters tread ozone squiggles,
strike white silhouettes.
The deepening above is outer space.
Beneath me, a wooded island is a negro hairdo,
receding to the sea's wrinkled-skin march.
Later, irrigation channels form a regimental, pleated tunic.
The brown worms are rivers, the dots and oblongs, habitation,
while the sun slips below its own blood,
till grey brains of moisture tinge golden.
In the darkness these forms live on,
soundless electricity prints the puffy membranes;
they nudge each other in restless sleep.
I reawake over a jewelled coastline
expanding to car molecules, jumping shortening synapses;
the pulse of man's work – warming the globe's wires.
Enlarging to diamond columns and artified star-ways;
the city's living skeleton, a lego game and meccano set
frightening in its continuum,
its reassertion over another failed escape.
My plane lands, abrupt and crestfallen …
taxiing slavishly.

# Derwent Water (Cumbria)

Treading the crust of iced-lake shore
our lungs swallow our bodies
and the fells climb the sky.
While the water cracks under wind's warming sweep,
the marsh is probed with phantom trunks –
and a sheep's black head
is betrayed by its nervous eye.
The glassy spurs ahead dovetail now in a double image,
and smiling, speechless,
we find the footprints of another.

## II

Hauling up the forest slope nothing escapes the crystal gaze
every sound enlarged in a virgin garden.
At the summit – the pines stand spidery shiver-guard,
clouds and mountain joined, the sun has abdicated,
the heart soaring idiotically –
colder than cold until we stop.

## III

With flush of returning blood at lower ground re-gained
we kiss the tremble on each other's lips.
Emerge, awake, at the deep-welled stream
sprung free in thaw's frenzy
to which we two, alone – bend to drink
humble in our interruption.

# A Day Late

The gorge was high, wide, wet-green. A perfect place for ambush – though smug-serene was the piper playing to the falls' roar…and more slippery then the steps to the stone-gagged stream.

'You a Macdonald by any chance?' the old lady yelled from the cottage wreathed with green moss and a lamb's morse code bleating.

The man ran on – a Long Tom Colley – clutching the woman's neck-wrenched hen under his coat; stooping breathless then for the fence-wire. The man cursed the hill ahead, receding and deepening in its betrayal, his feet now sunk in sheep dung – and the heights ahead soon to blank with fog.

It's a perfect place for an ambush, he thought.

As surely as the starless night, the lump of farmhouse beyond the last gate, the place where his gang should have been waiting – is speechless.

For this is Glencoe. The man is a day late. He had stolen a chicken for their supper. And his whole family lay dead indoors.

## Nativity (Bethlehem, 1994)

Strictly, only certified Christians can enter
the Church of the Holy Sepulchre.
But downstairs, at the manger site,
past the burial place of children killed by Herod,
the usual video and flashbulb clamour arose,
the venue jammed beyond civility by Egged-coach pilgrims.
Only when a Greek mass started,
and a woman led the starkly naked, a cappella,
was the avaricious multitude stilled.

Inevitably, the original Christmas comes to mind.
I could all but hear the cattle, lowing,
the infant starting to life on the straw,
where shepherds and their flocks outside
would see the brightest star appear over that place.
On that occasion no less than this windy, wintry day
a multitude could be as quiet as one person thinking
if its members were joined by a common purpose.

And wherever the stone-throwers,
the bombers, the tanks and the gunships
are defending anyone's sovereignty,
or justifying the rape of mothers, sisters, daughters, virgins,
before bound-men in the name of occupation
even in the fleeting peace of this mini-Berlin
and it's 'practical' apartheid,
they surely would never have cause to violate
this stable. This citadel
where God's journey back to man found earth.

# Regarding Cézanne

The wind in the pines.
The movement of light in the wind in the pines.
The figures of boys
running through the blue shadows
of the mist's ephemera
under the uncrossed bridges of childhood.
Was it all just a buzz in his brain?
Cézanne could not tell us, unburden
in parables and gossip like his friend, Zola.
He could not speak his pain
of the fear that was only the fear of him
in the faces of others,
that stubbornness that turned him repeatedly from company;
hiding his smile behind a storm of beard.
Some feared him mad.
That he was capable of rage and suicide –
but never that shy, uncomplaining woman who posed for him.
And always it was his eyes
that failed and yet made him.
That made three sight planes in one picture, logical.
Like the cracked vision of an age;
the era of electricity and steam power and Eiffel Tower
where, what had been taken for granted
could never be true again.
Maybe he just didn't want to paint really
but putting a skewed geometry on canvas
was a way to mitigate insanity.

The best of Cézanne was always deaf to change
yet made its own way from the clumsiness of including people
even as origins finally demanded order.
He died of pneumonia after one walk alone too many,
hunting, who knows?
A glimpse of where he began.
Of that feeling that never failed
when he only wanted to be
that wind through the pines,
that exquisite, forest-green;
that beckoning, indefinable ikon of St Victoire.
The reality of light moving the trees.
That vision of bathers lighting shadows.
A boy's damning terrestriality – dreaming only of wings
under the uncrossed bridges of childhood.

# Jonestown

from a girl among the Chosen

We won't yet give sex to the Boss
and he sends us away, saying,
'You want to injure our unity.'
But we will not leave him – that's plain.
Everything outside is twisted.
Everyone's afraid.
Everyone reports on everyone else.

Peasants work the earth
while the Boss sits in comfort before an air conditioner
and people are spying on each other.
This passing out of the brown liquid in plastic cups,
it was only a drill, wasn't it?
We each had a small bag packed for the Hereafter
but that was only insurance.

The air-raid sirens are blaring.
The Boss is screaming,
'The authorities are closing in!'

We kneel and repeat to ourselves,
we have no possessions,
we have no curiosity,
we do as we're told.
We have only the Family of All.

We cannot leave or we'll be struggled.
Have to do the dirtier jobs,
every privilege banished to a dream.
Love, of course is All Around.

The Boss is screaming,
'The Government is hunting us down
the FBI, the CIA,
the people who call us Communist,
urge us to surrender – now!'

'The time has come,' the loudspeakers blare.
It's only a drill
in the old way – isn't it?
We feel the weight of our bags to make sure.

We sway with spots before our eyes.
Insight always comes with hyperventilation.

I take up the paper cup, close eyes and drain the brown liquid.

'We come from the Heavenly Father!'
We stand up and shout
'We shall endure over all!'
My voice. His voice. All voices
coming from a long way off

above these statues of the praying – now frozen.

I hear the sirens coming towards us

and, somehow, I begin to run towards them…

Jonestown was the site of the People's Temple set up by sect leader the Rev. Jim Jones in Guyana in the 1970s.

# A Clear Night in Memphis (Alexander's Destination)

The blackness behind him
was always the enemy
while he, white-heat on his charger,
portraying wisdom frightening
to elders and the earthy,
was so furious, in battle.
The final opponent for the self-proclaimed
Son of Jesus, lay elsewhere,
husbanded by that half-brother, Ptomely
who was shunned by the mother witch.
Ptomely, the shyest of the court panthers,
the official food taster to the powerful,
soothed yet the mortal temper of the God.
Only in the silent wondering grief
of multitudes in the shadow of Babel
was the half-brother's calumny made safe.
Zeus, Alexander, God anyway
would have his will appeased.
An unvanquished legend
preserved, mummy-like,
borne in a chariot gold;
camel train under salty chill of moonless heavens,
to a seat in the land of Two Tribes.
The playground of Pharaohs;
the source of classical permanence, posterity,
an appointment with the ancients at Siwa
had been set in spirit and stone.
A Macedonian conqueror
would be interned offshore.

The Other of him
would wheel among the stars;
the winking bubbles in an old man's glass of wine.

Blood only with blood may unify.

## Goya's Blind Guitarist

No one knows his name.
He mumbles only a request for alms.
His face is not important,
hidden, banally, under his hat.
We are meant to study instead, his audience:
the frilled and stockinged businessman,
the ostler,
the tough guy from the tavern,
the children playing on the grass,
the lady with her mantilla extended…

they are each seeing different things
in the song of the man
who cannot see,
who can only reach out
with his involuntary urge…
who can only play what he feels,

and ends up – if he's lucky,
at the end of each day,
with a few thrown coins.

# After Mabo

Is this the way we want things to be?
Under the black/white law
only half of us may ever understand?
And not only those who see it as a fightback.
Aboriginal theft, of whiteman sacred sites,
mining and woodchip holy places,
resort development rarities,
tourist-dollar sacrosanct shrines –
all once gleams in sacred nature's eyes.

No one thought we'd have to go this far:
no more freewheel, no more ride roughshod,
no more selling overseas without restraint,
no more compensation without complaint.
No more 'I walk the land and it is mine.'
Can the black/white Law still bring me back,
like Eddy, to burial in his first, true one place?
troubled soul no more to roam?

No one conceived we'd have to go this far.
Nailing demarcation labels, like seismic notations
out of Capetown, on the chequerboard landscape.
Dot com signposts in an arid continent.
But we must all make of this Mabo
a document living and historical.
In the age of the lawyer dynasty, the litigation arena,

the claims quadrangle, of participants dumb to one another
beyond the argument –
anyone, outside legislation, beyond reconciliation
will simply *not* be on the map.
OK, then. Welcome to the settling resetting of Australia.
Tell, in a treaty, how you really want it to be – now.

# Night on Mount Ann

South-west Tasmania

The moon has not moved.

A bout of shivering has reawakened me.

Here I am, in shirt sleeves,
on the area's highest mountain,
with a timing delay on my camera,
hoping to record the effect
of heaven's light on the fellow peaks
bathed in post-midnight glow
far below…

That excuse/idea had become my tunnel vision,
assuming I'd need no other nourishment, shelter.

For an instant, memory,
webs stickily close once more –
food, wine and argument,
a lover's body curving to make one with my own –
then the shivering starts again.

Once more I lean against the rock;
better varicose veins than sleep swallowing, suffocating, me.

Yet, the moon has not moved.

I wait, like an assassin, to pull the shutter's trigger;
time's up on this exposure.

## Ballerina

Ballerina
spinning light,
for whatever reason
we explored,
the darkness of our shared space,
it was never
to break
your wings.

# Smiley 2

Echoed in the New, wider world
was the story of the little boy lost in the bush:
'at 19 we were sent to Nam, sent to sew a Viet meadow…'

It was held firm, steady –
this man's poisoned cup.
His still-civil paranoia made him laugh erratically
and forget his awful teeth when he smiled.
That's what had earnt him his nickname.
'Take a sip,' he said, gazing at the faraway light of the Anzac bridge…

Thirty-six hours later – he tried to hang himself from it
and fell to a banal splatter in the traffic;
the knot to his society's latest war shrine, severed.

He'd come back to the city
to 'give' his old lady back to her mother,
knowing the noose tightening
was the collar he could not share.
The steady eye behind the damp handshake,
the furious smoking of cigarettes,
told you his doubt was over.
That the walk to the end,
the walk across the South Asia minefield,
the stepping out into the air
above the Anzac bridge traffic,
were but parts in a plan ready to make flesh.

That rush of knowing the score,
that accelerating arc
in a pill that whispered his name;
that leopard, in the hallway of his insomnia,

that's what he couldn't let go of.
Before it sprang
into the night.

Thinking, after one meeting,
that I had known him,
I took up Smiley's cup
and placed my reason there.

# Thameside Cohorts (early 1980s)

## The First Path

In the beginning was the magic
of first discovery but not the knowing,
in tentative journeys from a half-house in Ealing.
The crowded, damp High Street was the first view,
the friendliness of the red buses,
autumn's vermillion dusks splashing house-face and misty common.
Later came the forays to Richmond's deer park,
Kensington's sunken gardens,
Kew's incredible greens and yellows –
but it was not absorbing you, city.
I was possessed by fantasy.
Failing to grasp a constant,
I sought the night's tourist face;
West End shows, Piccadilly cinema – Hot Pot dining,
waiting for Convent Garden – ballet in the Purcell Room,
but it was Her ethereal other-world –
this mysterious stranger who coolly controlled.
The ardour of my self-illusion only exposed my charlatanry:
my rabbits that would not jump, my doves that could not fly.
Till the fantasy ended.
She married a man of God.
I discovered Christ's Scarecrow.
For a poet's is seldom the privileged view.
Only the fragility
of first discovery but not the knowing
though nothing is ever
how I was told it would be.

## The City

Chasing the thump of your hunted step: here is the city!
Wesley Graveyard, Finsbury Circus
Moorfields, Bank and Monu-ment!
It pushes you on, pushes you on!
Ages revolve through the slumbers of years
wandering the maze, beyond the Roman walls:
Wesley Graveyard, Finsbury Circus,
Moorfields, Bank and Monu-ment!
Between Gray's Inn and Bunhill Fields,
layers of church bells, bones of scattered villages:
buried fossils of plague and fire.
Wesley Graveyard, Finsbury Circus,
Moorfields, Bank and Monu-ment.
Till Greater, Inner and Outer become Inner, Greater and Outer.
It pushes you on –
a river through woods and a temperate climate
ground down by human race, struggle for breath –
Wesley Graveyard, Finsbury Circus
Moorfields, Bank and Monu-ment!

## The Hunger

Dirty corridor-mile – stretches before my mop:
it is 6 a.m.
Once more I am cleaning the Guildhall.

I live in a squat in Bethnal Green
on a triangle of abandoned Victoriana.
The people here wear battledress
and flit between the bars of wind.
A siren pierces the nerves in a schoolyard,
while back of the barber shop, boxing gym,
the thick-necked scouse swaggers,
towel-flicking, telling tales of Turpin's Aldgate.
As dawn stalks abandoned minefield
of broken-down shopfront,
rag and junk sold off outside the Blood and Bone.
A Stepney sharp is shouting, 'Cocks! Cocks! A pound a pound!'

Dirty corridor-mile stretches before my mop – back and
forth, back and forth:
in my mind I am picking over old trousers,
tongues of boots in Brick Lane.
From nowhere comes the smell of bagels:
the rising smile of an Indian girl.

## Wallwords

Bobbie Sands was killed by Maggie Thatcher
NF NF NF NF NF NF
No one wins wars, you can only fight them
Why can't we stop knowing how to hate?
Start learning how to love!
What does it mean to me?
Some of the wall-words you see,
Stumbling home
Lonely heart dead of night.
NO RAZOR

## End of Form

Grey midday
toll of school bell
poppy in the minefield,
a war-child's war-child legacy.
Echoes mocking in a quadrangle game,
the left-last-year
now forever-unemployed
become council flat gangs,
terrorists' apprentices;
the joke that kills,
nuclear mutants: the feeling before the fact.

You've all seen the bollocks
now it's the Clash of the Specials;
but how could these rut-runners be a nation's children?
And for whom then do those sirens sing?
Poverty's factory animals
bums bare against the barbed wire?

Blood leaves an indelible graffito:
history class
is in these rioting streets
today.

## Saturday Park

Windy and bare – over and over
the Whippy van refrain
vomiting cheer.
All the paint stripped off the trees.
The fallow deer stand cemented.
Taste of metal in the mouth could just be hunger.
Plans abandoned – shops all closed
telephones all broken
pull out a piece of cardboard from a skip
you can't walk past without looking in.
Inside, an old drunk asleep.
Fish-eyes in the gutter, smell
where the market happened – yesterday.

## The River

The river has reported for duty again;
a pipe in an old man's mouth
above the slugs of brown.
The ravens still guard the Tower:
swooping down from Money Canyon
to peck at the red neck of the needy,
with the chords of brave St Paul bellowing, 'Praise Him!
Praise Him!';
the fist thrust back at Hitler's Blue Max,
to keep Lincoln's Inn safe
for the Law Courts' granite, medieval souls.

The ravens still guard the Tower
as their cousins wire up on white-spirit breakfast cocktails
at their bedsits in Embankment Gardens.
And a CND rally fights its way up the Strand.
While Barbican is a busy death of inner-city living dream:
the ducks feed on Coke cans in the artificial lake
under the fake waterfall.
And the river is on its feet.
It's the flow to and fro
of business-army suits and ties.

# Faces

The art of subterfuge was my native land's insidious gift:
should I try on these expressions of London?
The Mayfair door porter in Regency costume,
the breathing sculpture of a Palace soldier,
sunglasses and moustache smile the Bankcard Garner steak,
while a black man in a fez clutches an *A to Z*,
skinheads kick a bottle into Mare Street,
reggae rabbis of Hackney are funking Thatcher
and a hermit in Poplar is decaying.
A backpacker is at a crossroads in Euston
and a Cockney swears in Smithfield's market:
sheep's balls fill his hands like grapes.
Cannibalism is now civilised,
but fifty journalists in a smoke-filled room
only came for the beer,
while overcoats are laying out tramps
under Charing's Cross.

## Identity

Scarecrow was a spiritual man.
He was the troubadour, the urchin-gypsy gleeman.
He came unto the frightened.
He came unto the curious.
He came unto the distracted and the displaced.
He came unto the pretenders,
smelling of the weather and the earth,
carrying stones in his pocket
smoothened by rough trespass,
corks and lucky charms – the sweets for children.
He came with the storm-blown seed of many journeys.
He came and he entranced.
The thief of the mind
he came and they made friends with his hollowness.
He panhandled and philandered
and his wit cut wicked at the blushes of those older women.
For his flower was flush for the feintings of nubile fancies.
And birds flew into their soul.
For fertility was his gift:
the mask he wore.

# Sex

Yet it was a sacrament to me…
Candlelit – all flesh looked holy.
I was a costumed explorer voyaging sun-hidden places.
A body became an island;
my lips blew ships – into its mantle of hair,
and skin flowed with skin
in the night cut with cries
til the bursting and the joining
in perfume our honey made,
the murmur of our waves
trapped in the pearl of the ear.

# Character Reference From a French Lady Living in Streatham

So ho! You *do* come down out of your tower, dictator! You mock my seriousness about emotion and my taste in films. You're bored by my conversation and my dress sense. You hurl insults at my astonished being – you make arrangements then break them with excuses. You trade patience for foul and complex phrases. You get angry when I'm late and I don't like kissing in public. You won't let me come to your place. You dismiss my fears and health worries and fly away shouting. What do you want of me – and why do I care? *Merde!*

## Vigil

Cruel then that the beckoning game
was the memory that endured,
for I was a fugitive finding fugitives,
shunned by the glow-worm eyes
of the museum's fact corpse:
Tussaud's no-blink taunt of fame.
For there was no change here
no…discovery,
but the wonder of hallucinations in mind's winter:
Belgravia's green squares bisecting streets of fretted iron.
The permit holders rent them
as compost heaps for their diamond dogs.
While the cops patrol with talkie-porkie –
keeping it cool for the quo.
And the geriatrics hover
power-jewelled in an early autumn,
and the antique poodle
shivers fear to pee.

## Shelter

I am lonely now in the parks.
Camden calls to soothe my broken wings.
I am carrying a book of poems
in the pentameter zone of Jack Straw's castle.

Dickens lived in Bayham Place
when London was still a long way off.
Keats and Shelley walked Hampstead Heath;
in my shell-shocked snow
a stream claws at the roots for life.
While winds of argument blew through parlour coteries;
and my circle waited here, too,
objects of their discarded art poured newborn
into a room of eager ears,
whose ghosts nested in the ceiling
for future Gods to apprehend.

Each sunup I crossed myself at the sight of Saint Pancras
hanging angel-crazy in gasworks summer field.
Yet how do these trees grow to caress our prickly walls?
Like Roman Way runs by Pentonville Prison,
like friendship is an albatross:
half carried by and half carrying me.

# Option

On the Fairlea Council estate
a door bangs black with grime.
Kids kick a ball.
A slumped body in the courtyard
is drunk or dead.
No place this for the African ladies
laughing by the supermarket, Saturday noon.
No coin for the trip home
as Nazi conductor barks, 'Tickets please!'
And I am reduced to a stumble
through kamikaze old-lady solidarity in Tesco's.
Though singing from the corner pub
floating through bedroom Sunday haze
relieves the night – premonition of holocaust –
corridors stained by children's splattered faces.
I am released
back to the market of no-option –
second-hand books, beds, overcoat, life.
The future vision palpable in trembling blood of now
but reactions picked at random
from my fifteen personalities.
In this at least I am consistent.
Vow of no responsibility, obligation
the entry form blank of signature
for the necessary game:
I do not make the rules.

## Perspectives

From Highgate Hill I can see the Euston PO.
Centrepoint, the Tower, St Paul's.
Far to the east a thick forest haze.
Hard to believe London was once anything
but kerbstone, factory, flat
cringing stick-treed park and winter.

Into the Savoy sea of lights – a Daimler glides,
stiff arms untouchable and brandy breath
still dress the porch of the Wig and Pen.
But the city is no longer an obstruction.

And would that I had wandered these streets
as the young Cook did – before salt swam into his blood,
before he married the sail and fate cast him
the telescope and the ship's wheel.
Before he set out on the globe's great curve
to the new planets in the Pacific.
And would England have been as far from him
when the clubs rained down in the friendly Sandwich isles
as my home now appears to me?
For home was the name he had to give England,
yet is that land I have left any less strange
than this labyrinth heavy with man's strivings?
Or my awed mind less transported here than the explorer's,
confronting nature's elemental stirring:
that which goes on in spite of man.
The Bush's covert universe.

### Five fifteen

And with us on this crowded platform
was this guy who looked strange,
strutting up and down the platform
like a mannequin at a rehearsal.

He walked up to one person after another,
smiled at them, like a clown.
They each stared at him, but did not say anything.
He walked up to me and smiled.
I stared at him but I did not say anything.

He raised his arms and yelled.
We all stared at him but we did not say anything.
We were all holding-in angry, waiting for the bloody train.
We stared at each other then, but we did not say anything.

Then the train was coming.
The strange guy sighed.
He walked right up to the edge of the platform.
He was solemnly staring at something in front of the train
as it approached
and, before he jumped,
I knew, again.
Despite all our fine words we would say to our conscience
it was we others who were powerless.

We, who had failed.

## Traffic

The traffic roars on.
A man stands outside a massage parlour in Eversholt Street.
His head convulses back and forth.
He is saying something only he can understand.
He stares at the sky.
His head convulses back and forth.
He is saying something
only he can understand;
haranguing the sky.

The traffic roars on.

## Story of Bozo

Bozo here. Bozo there.
His name on a wall – everywhere.
From Shoreditch to Camden Town – Archway to Streatham common,
Hampstead to Maida Vale – Elephant and Castle, Earls Court.
Then – nothing. Not a sign. Taggers increasing but Bozo lost from light…
Until a new lettering appears in a strange childish hand.
Halting. Doubtful – no slick trademark like Banksy would become…
Just the news… 'Bozo is in stir.'

## Resolution

London you are only my second mistress.
How can I speak of you as final?
When how little and useless I appear,
but how fearful of my mortality!
And how do I see myself
from in front of myself?
An ape pawing at his mirrored image:
a stuffed death, awaking spasmodically
into uncomprehended dream.
How…can I see myself?

Only through this one now with me,
watching and responding
with child's smile on wisdom's joy.
For only with this one
is there the capacity, the caring;
for only with this one
can I make ever-new
the help we can give each other.

## Underground

Cover again the city surface
with the tracing of the finger
on the Underground map.
Pace the platform
while walls blabber dreams, ambitions.
And what is the riddle
running from hollow stomach to bulging head?
The plans we cannot buy.
The faces we must not touch.
The hands that will never join.
The smiles we do not believe.
The formation we will not own.
The motion we cannot stop.

On the train, the doors suck shut
to onrush of black:
impossible, incalculable noise and speed –
and transport – to another world?
Only another name-relic of vanished past
and the billboards ranting on
their dreams for rent.

## Surrender

The thrill/fear of my voyage out
belongs now to others.
And impossible that I should think of re-arriving there
like the native's first coming
of sixty thousand years before.

The lessons learnt away will serve me feeble
in unlocking my homeland's stony secrets.
She will deny and deny – yet remain: irresistible.
For my potential with her will never be tested,
filling like a well – of water I can never drink.
Perhaps the sailors who ferried forth my kind
two hundred years ago
drank of the sea's foamy ether like I must imbibe
the modern city's brash and resolute air.
Sailors, who left dreams in discarded boats,
surprised to be not surprised
their courage growing, guileless:
they were merely dwelling in that no-time,
before the stillness
made its binding shapes about them.

# Eyes of the Castaway

Cabin boy Jan Pelgrom de Bye, along with able seaman Wouter Loos, was put ashore by Captain Pelseart of the doomed ship *Batavia* on a remote part of the WA coast in 1629 after being judged a participant in a mutiny following the ship's foundering upon a reef in the Abrolhos Islands. The following is his solo testament to his surroundings.

Sheeeoor! Sheeeooor! Sheeeoorr!

Nothing will ever happen.

Nothing will ever happen.

Nothing more will *ever* happen!

Once a jolly sail-or oh.

Set the boom spar for the south-west!

'It's not a reef! It's just the shine of the moon!'

'Land-ho! Land-ho!'

The waves keep comin in, coming.

But I must stop *listening* to them!

And the image of the Captain's hand.

Hitting me in the face…

'You'll go stark raving mad man!'

It's all over out there now.

It's all over out there now.

It's all *over* out there now!

Sheeeoor! Sheeeoor! Sheeeoorr!

And the gulls watching me, watching.

Hang out in the breeze aha!

Once a jolly sail-or oh.

Set the boom for the south-west!

'It's not a reef! Just the shine of the moon!'

'Land ho! Land ho!'

The water coming in, coming…

Why can't I stop, why can't I?

I am an animal! A bird animal!

Nature's Creation just like them!

Nothing will ever happen.

Nothing will ever happen!

Nothing *more* will ever happen!

The captain's hand smacking down

'You'll go stark raving mad man!'

Sheeeoor! Sheeeoor! Sheeeoor!

Why can't I stop!?

# Liar-byrd

He crow-croaked like a politician
and she lowered her head in a spasm of concern.
He racketed like a thrush.
He cursed and dipped like a sorcerer
sent from God…
She blinked back all expectation…
Now he fluttered instead, some deranged butterfly;
a model angling from a catwalk
in-camera dementia.
She peeked out of the corner of one eye…
He mistook it for a goading –
a timidity on demand.
He rustled his chain mail like a scrub turkey,
hectoring, hee-hawing, braying;
a real-estate developer boning up,
honing in on closure.
She mewed – like reality
taking a cold shower.
He made himself invisible
in a patch of palms.
The air thrummed with electricity.
She wanted a holiday from questions but
found feet stuck fast in failed flight…
He landed: 'thump!' before her;
a fanfare of trumpets.
She scolded from instinct
but cringed becomingly soon after.
He leered over like a vulture,
though his song dripped with jewels; gewgaws.

He lay in a sauna
beckoning her to join him in the hot tub.
She became the prim schoolgirl:
her dad was making an improper invitation.
She was snooty in her drudgery.
He erupted into singing
all birds of the rainbow.
His frame expanded into a 1,000 wingspans.
She felt herself surrounded;
by mirror-multiple doubles,
reflections from a fibrous universe.

He begged her to accept everything and be absorbed
but only silence replied.

He ran from one side of his
argument to the Other;
audience, antennae and hero,
perpetrator and jury, all.
Two sides of one coin, spy to spy
in brightness, dazzling.
He stretched. He sung her like the howl of a hundred bees;
a freight train, his vision brimming –

and a kookaburra and his mate
suddenly fell, laughing, from a tree.
Rosellas carved lumps from the twilight
as they swept past; rollerblades on the air
in their breathless errands.

This gave him pause.

Opportunity for introspection.

The day of the tournament was closing
signalling yet one more joust with Time itself.
The female lyre-bird registered her exhaustion
and was all mousy humility but…
as he came near –

'Liar!' She hissed. 'Liar!'

No, he had not tweaked her mind after all.

'Liar!'

Stepping daintily free of his web –
she stood cemented if not compliant –
staring through him who was darkening, shrivelling
before the shades of evening…

She felt strong.
She would not move away.

This was *her* space!

# The Railway System (Another View)

The Sydney public would like to advise
City Rail that the object of a timetable
is to have trains actually appear, and adhere to it.
We encourage every effort be made
to achieve that outcome.

Please note that for your security the Sydney public
regularly patrols this station to check
whether overdressed, ex-con, security part-timers are lurking
with no intent to work. Those persons are reminded
the public is paying their wages and their service can be
terminated at any time.

The Sydney public would like to advise that if a given train
has not arrived 5 minutes after the scheduled time
it can no longer take
any responsibility for what may happen to station amenities
and equipment as a result. It will eat, drink and smoke
and throw rubbish
wherever it pleases in the ensuing indeterminate interval.

The Sydney public wishes to advise State Rail
it did not have the time to wait
for the forthcoming service (now finally approaching).
There are therefore no passengers to now collect.
The Sydney Public apologises for any inconvenience caused.
And thanks you
for your patience and cooperation.

The Sydney public wishes to advise State Rail
that this station has been closed by popular dissent.
Would all would-be protesting train drivers
and station personnel
once their trains have finally arrived, or have not been cancelled,
leave quietly thereafter for any unemployment office,
wherever, that is prepared to receive them.
Please note that Service testimonial and referee statement forms
are out of print because of the current heavy demand for them.

Your crime is important to us. Please hold.

Thank you.

# Love's Analergy

Our goodbye tonight
was not happy.
The words we normally
dress ourselves with – to confirm
our separateness and parting –
would not come.
Instead, something had to be torn away.

I woke at 3 a.m.
with all these little bites
on my feet and lower body.
I found chocolate in the fridge
and seemed to think
that eating it, as an antidote, would work.

That sleep was a ship
pulling away from shore – and you were on it.

Last night, at your door
our mouths kept framing words of farewell
like faces at a porthole.

Only our eyes were hearing and speaking.

And my hands make sounds now

scratching at my itch.

# Part Two

# Meeting Point

I am pastel
I am dusk
nosing around the forms
of figures working on a body
in the back of an ambulance:
the 13-year-old vessel
I've just, apparently, departed.

The grainy recall of a car grille
as it rises up out of the ether
misting into a parchment of echoes.

*Nature seems to be fuzzing in and out*
*whisper of the water wheel*
*figures poking here and there*
*my mother's late-afternoon languor*
*(where is she?) a calmness*
*my elder brother's shouts/cries*

The grainy recall of a car grille
meeting a 13-year-old boy
who had chased a cricket ball onto the road;
the body flung up in cartwheels/wings
impact of his landing: 'He's dead! He's dead!'

I am pastel
I am dusk
*Coming from a long way off*
yet this new planet always looks familiar.
The white-robed men continue their putting back together.

I go from one witness, bystander, to the other
even the country neighbours who've run up to look
from stopped cars:
'He never had a chance!'
'And where is the driver? Was he speeding?'
'Someone has been taken away by a doctor
to get an injection for the shock, I guess.'
Now here's the father, Jack, the daughter and the 8-year-old:
'God, what does *he* know of it?'

'Our game of cricket is interrupted by this? Some stranger
who was struck! Where's Danny gone?'

The grainy recall of a car grille charging onwards.
*Now it appears smaller, now larger*
I am pastel.
But the vessel's new entity will laugh off
the repercussions. He's been this way before.
*I am dusk and, somehow, velvet*
I must get aboard before they take him away
to the hospital. Not the morgue.
What new motives will I be able to pass on?
What wouldn't be preferable to the mortal end?
*Calmness in the eternal dusk*

I was riding with that car grille
and now I have found him.
His future, here, is my mission.

# From the navigator of the Enola Gay

on the 60th anniversary of VJ Day

It was a beautiful day.
We were in sight of the target from 25 miles out.
We opened the hatch – all systems go
and dropped Little Boy.
It took about 41 seconds and at about 1,800 feet
the flash came.
The wave rose up and hit us, shook the plane
to its foundations.
We couldn't even see the city below
the released energy made such a cloud.
There was no doubt the bomb had worked.
The mission was a success.
We were in a war
and – I don't know
to bring about the end of any war
people have to die.
I won't say we were just following orders
but it was not our decision.
The Japanese were already defeated
but their military was so stubborn
they would have kept going until there was nobody left.
Under the same conditions
in the same situation
I would do it again.
The persons in the streets of Hiroshima and Nagasaki
were in the same position
as the Japanese soldier, or the airman –
like we, the crew, were ordinary folks
when we went back home.

# Fraud of Reason

after German mountaineer Reinhold Messner

I laughed when the villagers
'mistook' my footprints in the snow for the yeti.
To them my 'demon' was merely
another part of living in an isolated community.
But on my next bivouac on the mountain
I was awoken by the brute's breath
hot against my cheek…

I fled from a following shadow
which lay in wait
while I sought shelter in a deserted hut –
then it began to break down the door.
A monster with a human's cunning.
This was *too* much!

I found myself in a blizzard
praying the night might never fall again.
I was blindly following
a shape through the snow,
paralysed, submissive to its every step…
When the hairy back suddenly turned:
it revealed the face of a man.

My mind froze but my legs did not.
I ran down from the unreachable summit
of my quest,
feeling the weight of those staring, scattered villagers.
I was roaring and foaming in my fear…
Looking, yes – like a monster.

## Space – Are You?

Ah…space…at last we are alone!
I've been meaning to ask you…
the pilot of all these potentially wayward craft
in this black endlessness.
Are you the future?
Because – when I close my eyes
I feel myself hurtling forward.
But, at other times – are you the past?
Because, when I close my eyes
I feel time rushing back
to a place we met before.

When we were not yet rock
…not quite metal!

What are we now?

Space.
Can we really be
the only creatures that recognise you –
rather than just react to you?

Did we ever think when we started out
we would end up like this?
When we close our eyes…
When we close…

Space…
are you God?

# Stare

A memory from polio at 17 months

The door some way off opens

I am lost in some sort of fever…

I feel someone looking down at me in my cot.
Surprised – I stare back
at the stare.

Stare.
Don't look away.
Stare.
Don't feel weak.
Stare.
Don't give up.
Their eyes boring in…
Stare.
Keep the eyes steady.
Stare.
Don't give up.
Don't look away.
Stare.
Keep the eyes like metal –
on those eyes that bore in.
Keep the eyes locked
steady.
Till they look away.

You are here.
You are
here.
*Make* those eyes look away.
They will come back to stare again.
Don't give in – don't feel weak.
Stare.
Stare.

Some way off…
The door has closed.

The fever creeps back to cover me.

I cannot close my eyes

## At Burke's Grave

One hundred and forty years after

It was not summer's fire
that consumed him and his men,
it was the thirst-slaking bounty of winter.
On a day like this, perhaps,
when wood-doves 'cooed' at dusk,
pelicans threshed in the brown artery,
crows fussed, distracted, among the skeletons of twigs
and a green finch sung of water's gentle glide.
These riches Burke and his men could not see
like the advice of those 'shadows' the natives.

The expedition party had done the hard part.
Bridged the land to the marsh gulf.
Tho crazed by the morass of saltwater dead-ends,
it proved there was a finale you could come back from.
The men had achieved the physical facts.
But Burke's fate had not been made Lore;
the faith of those back home, wanting, like ashes.
Fame's depraved mistress had still to be assuaged.

Burke, you died malnutrite, no matter what riches
the black brothers brought to trade.
Tasting nothing but that denied sweet poison
you died broken, a ghost already, inside a skull.

'Leave me here with my gun,' your voice hoarsened,
'while morning grows warm – and demons of the mind fade.'

As these same trees now sigh with desires unspent,
I smile and feel my spirit rise – to shake hands
with an Aboriginal companion.
To reach, for the loaf of bread, we made together.
To gather the fishes of the pelicans,
to accept the jewels of Tucker's terrorists, the parrots,
falling from the echoing sky.

# Spain, Are You Here?

early 1980s

Pushing on into *pays basque generale*,
towns of TV stick high-rise – the odd estranged cupola,
political slogans: *Fronte! Para Independencia!*
The terrain steepening into heavy industrial.
The province wants its own destiny instead of
paying for tourism in the south.
Every so often a stream through the smoky hills -
they write it with their blood.

SPAIN, ARE YOU HERE?
In the hills and plains of Castille.
La Mancha – where the helmeted scarecrow
once led his plump, faithful conscience.
In the orange-brown soil, in Soria,
site of old Numantia where, for 14 years, from 133 BC,
four thousand men and women
defied Scipio of Rome and his sixty thousand soldiers,
until, surrounded, and having eaten their horses,
their dead companions and having cast lots to eat themselves,
they set fire to the town
in response to a final, Roman command to surrender.
Every surviving Numantian threw himself on those flames.
And Garcia Lorca wrote an essay about the *duende*
an undiabolic demon that possesses the Spanish character.

SPAIN, ARE YOU HERE?
On this suffocating old train – east of Alicante.
Passing men and donkeys under toil,
tolled by the village church bell
until, hungry only for itself, the land choked them out,
discarding even the birds as hangers-on,
turning pastures to flat dust bowls,
making broken and directionless the roads,
hardening into hot-steel, industrial towns,
spare, wide outposts of American Old West,
with grim survivors hauling hearse-heavy suitcases
under wide-brimmed hats.

Ahead, a plateau breaks the torpor –
those white cubes must be the Capital.
An oasis in the long, flat tray of land –
*Ole Madrid! Ole!*
But first, in low-rise preface, a shanty town:
children running between sheet-iron humpies
jumping awry under brave washing lines,
running up to the train to dare
challenge the unstoppable machine;
the desperate, unpublicised, pathetic Spain
that Franco cauterised but did not quench.

SPAIN. ARE YOU HERE?
Time tricks you in this country.
People staying up so late – lights on the doorsteps
in each little village – families' dark vigilance
accents the affect of your running.
The bus's honking beams charging through blackness,
mocked by the face of the yellow half-moon.
Above, the Plateau – where the four Fates appeared before Goya
in the season of the witch –
the procession drags huge, grinning masks through the streets.
Yet, out of walls dressed in flowers, we run on
time capsuling itself 20, 30, a hundred night-times,
the next opening of the eyes and the next…
Time, we make up of our own reckoning, always wrong
and most of all in broken sleep.
Here, the day is the prison that must be waited out.
Night, the liberation of the soul and dreams.
It flees you, finally, with the tumbling screech of bats;
heads hanging from black trees.
A dawn you would have waited eternally for –
dropped from the bus, on the edge of town.

SPAIN, ARE YOU HERE?
In Cordoba
I walk to the river
a promenade throughu Roman ruins,
and between bridges, lovers walk,
or sit, stranded, over impasses, shied-from resolutions.
In Cordoba,
girls pass, photographing each other.

They are beautiful!
but in this country
how quickly they age.
In Cordoba
I reach my hotel
before I want to go home.
Join people 'fishing' oysters
from prepared water-bowls:
sucking out the sweet-sea flesh –
an ocean in my solitude.

SPAIN, ARE YOU HERE?
Late afternoon, Parc Maria Luisa, Seville,
the tropical plants form gardens
broken by ducks, ponds, pheasants
birds of paradise.
The ceramic benches' multicoloured tapestry
where fountains arch.
Its builders were Roman Catholics.
Lions and figurines haunt shaded alcoves,
sculptured groves yield *helada piratos'* ten-peseta scoops.
The white-dove square is manned by grit-sellers,
your mind lost in sheltered courtyards
washed with jasmine and Amelia.
It is an old saying here:
'yes, there is a summer wind
it comes but 4 times a day.'

The Plaza Espana
depicts Spain's recaptured Moorish provinces,
conquest of America,
spice from the East Indies:
but now the heads of state
of that golden three hundred years
gaze out at nothing
but the cost in lives.
And in the hostel that evening
what I took to be clapping hands
became the letting-go anger
of husband striking wife.
Their voices planed at each other – like cross-saws.
I cursed for sleep to come
siestas have upset my diurnal rhythm.
The kids just cried.

At 3 a.m., miraculously,
came the unmistakeable
rooftop pitter-patter.
I leaned out to gulp
those accidents of heaven,
the scant liquid jewels
from a star-filled sky.

SPAIN, ARE YOU HERE?
Old town Granada –
cathedral, university, chapels, wheel-barrow streets
festooned with bats and brats.
A beggar accosts me
point blank in the *heladeria*.
But I have the luck to find
an early-1900s tavern tipica,
with all the bullfight memorabilia:
graffiti, horns and heads
memory and testimonial,
the stories of famous men
who got drunk there.
Requiems to Garcia Lorca
a tragic, favourite son:
hanging hams and orange peelings
form torn, ragged shadows.
In the smoky lantern-light
this is a strange *otra mundo*
and the toothless old barman
sharpening knives,
years honing the fine line of corks;
he smiles
just in time!

## SPAIN, ARE YOU HERE?

A winding passage is steadily ascending
the ribbed lines of ill-fed foliage
are the lower reaches of the Alpajurras,
the Sierra's grey folds, bathed by the sun.
My destination is Orgiva:
a pensione next to a bus stop.
A tiny room at the corridor's end
contains bed and bedside bureau,
a washstand, a bucket,
a pitcher filled with water.
I draw the shade
on the cool stone floor
but the owner's wife is standing at the door -
beckons me to come and eat.

In the evening
following nooks and crannies in dry-wind dead ends
I find women sitting in concert
to their tiny children playing.
I walk with stealth
feeling the dull drills of their eyes.
The path to the sun's death
falls past tall cornfields,
tinkle of bells,
goatherd among olives.
The cars on the far road are murmuring to the summit.
Under the bridge where locals bathe
the silver of secret armies
jumps between the stones.

Dusk has rung down over the Communista café.
Limply, hangs, the sickle-and-star flag.
Who remembers 1937?
Not the kids running thru the rubble
or the dogs with their alert-moronic barking.
Midnight comes and goes
at drinks with the village's lovely old men
talking of what happened
to the Republican Traitors.
I watch the faces,
follow the eyes
sedated in my practised incomprehension.

But you must wait for many things in Spain
like I would that morning
for my one hour of sleep
watching the moon dull above the cupola
the air suddenly filling
with myriad scything birds.

SPAIN, ARE YOU HERE?
In Castell-Ferrero.
I met the evil eye on the beach
unable to swim the gritty water – much less sleep.
In my 'escape' sickness would befall me.
In the Spaniards' own resort any hostels were shut.
I saw a sign for '*Camas*' – a hole in the wall of a dining room,
the mother sewing in the corner,
the daughter resigned but dissatisfied.
I complained of thirst and she gave me
hot milk for an upset stomach.

Upstairs, the mother made up a bed.
The old man brought me food I couldn't eat.
I was hallucinating before the daughter, clasped her hand
against my forehead, whispering, '*Alma…alma mia.*'
She kept blowing into her clothing: '*Mucha calor – calor!*'
But the father called her off with a sad '*Ah – el hombre.*'
I turned to one side – purple rivers coursed my head.
Only *disprina* and *magnesio* from the *farmacia* could help.
Was I only sick in that bed?
And in a faraway land I found an incredible story Sarah had written.
I walked a familiar landscape with Alma:
'I knew you would not be happy with that other girl
She was too conscious of her own futility.'

SPAIN, ARE YOU HERE?
Marbella – has a film-star aura and high-rise gone crazy.
Miniature forests, water glistening thru trees from the highway,
villas and fine cars on ornate curving roads,
enclaves of retreat – for those with means. Yachts among the rocks.
A German girl said *nein* to sharing a pensione.
But a little old man at my last resort
said I could sleep on the balcony for half price.
The next day at dawn a Santander tourist clumsily befriended me.
I came back from the sands and the El Cordobe bar
to meet mealtime with my suddenly adoptive family:
Gonzalez and his wife, daughter Pilar and little Vanessa
and grandfather who raved out loud at unrehearsed moments.
At table: a beautiful alcohol-free wine from up north,
salads, ham and salami on bread – before the guapa Andaluz entertained.
She danced and sang – I had photographs taken hugging the others.

There were all the duty-free goods from Ceuta to show,
in-jokes and Gonzalez nudging me with wrinkled chocolate arms,
gesturing to Pilar to take my hands in another dance.
Vanessa curtsying through a forest of legs – as guitar tones enfolded –
I was quite at a loss to reply.
When the music stopped – it was Vanessa's bedtime.
I stepped out to a bar, meandered by the café maze
pilot lights of late-night ice cream stalls.
From a darkened doorway another song of the Spanish tongue shone –
a wall of murals of locals' stories fell down a narrow lane.

SPAIN, ARE YOU HERE?
In Algerciras, a busy, fly-blown, border cosmos
with Arab market, blind people, beggars,
where above the smelly Cafeteria Matilde
I get a room – while dark characters sell drugs in the bar below.
On the beach I met many travellers,
talked to them of Tangiers –
two bedraggled women with uppity accents
in the restaurant that evening had just 'escaped' Mali.
I saw many travellers.
You can no longer tell where they are from.
They have evolved, from a lifetime of moving.
They do not belong to any one country.
They are not of any one race.
They are travellers – they are a hunting people.
There is no choice in the matter.
No thought for the challenge or the course to pursue.

We are born to enquire, embrace and evade
no surge to the urge – the restless mind inside to indulge,
to be released from want and wanting.
You feel close to tears
waiting for the night to blink
corralled in someone's burning arms.

Spanish Proverbs:
'We live all our lives in the dark. We come out into the light
only at the hour of our death.'
'Always eat with your back to strangers. Only your spouse
should witness your table manners, blinded by her kindness.'
'Somewhere, traveller, we *all* have a Spanish mother.'

# Only the Men Are Dead

Looking over a battlefield from 1915

When the sun finally rose

no birds came near.

I was still there;

a sudden pall of lavender.

The eyes of the trees guarded those softly rustling greens and yellows;

veins in their uniform rows.

If I could have half-squinted, I'd have seen crosses.

The breeze when it came

had an oddly strident tune.

But now the trees are bare again

amid the grip of the lore

forming my resolve in enduring –

hell has not been decided for me –

much as the come and go of waves, machinery's blunt rhetoric.

I am a tombstone

and once more as the snows ease

more figures holding other flags are approaching

to chisel the meaning anew on these eyes

…buzz of flies.

## Season's End

Here's a book of photographs on the Rwandan genocide –
before and after.
Let's leave what happened to the bodies – to our imagination.
We're left with pictures of peoples' faces.
Some of the murderers for a fiat are now back in the community
among the relatives of the slain,
the unclouded eyes of the damaged but survived.
Here is the victim…and the killer
choose this one, choose that one…
which is which?
They look the same.
Look at those eyes – which one the guilty?
Which one the innocent, the survived?

Think of your town, your village, your suburb.
Think of pictures of people who live there.
Choose which one would kill you
if they were persuaded they had no choice
which one would not.
Even among the people you know…

We have to ask that question.
Which one would kill you?
Which one not?
Do they *look* the same?
Killer – or victim. Can you see the difference?
You choose.

Maybe you have come to be
like that old Rwandan woman
from whatever tribe
who walked out that early morning, strangely quiet;
into a mist she did not trust,
that had been weeping all night
from trees that have seen
what humans can do.

# The Face

Out of the subway
in the shadow of a huge gate
envoys from past times gathered
unaware they were miles
from the inner sanctum…

You can get a photograph of yourself
backgrounded
by a square that holds a million people.
Once out on that plateaued rifle range
you're shrunk down
to your true size: insignificance –
before the Red Star
and the Big Cat's portrait.

Is he still the ikon incarnate?
The last Official Emperor?
Or just a George Washington
who's stolen a 100 million apples/lives – all denied?
People are plying you with cries:
they still take your money and welcome you,
kite-shaped like birds – and bullets
but your ambitions are strictly earthbound.

You reach the city's gables, exhausted:
'Don't bring in cameras
Or other dangerous implements'
the sign warns.

Inside, the path
is swollen around squares in a symmetrical line
which again tactically skirts the labyrinth:
'Now – about these finials.'

At every succeeding layer upstairs, you are the Forbidden
easily picked off by the elaborate rifles of guards.
At the place they call
The Democracy Wall,
the occupant so divine in heaven's eye, scarifies,
when all you want him to show you is his facial recognition.
Someone is muttering into an iPhone,
'Reporting again – from Tiananmen.'

# New Eye Age

You're told by those who have it nowadays,
'cataract surgery is a doddle.'
'I'll believe it when I see it,' I retorted.
I wanted no expectations around: the 'cut' at 59.
Was I forcing myself not to visualise…?

On the bed before the anaesthetist, I hear,
'Tell me about your last holiday. Where is your favourite place?'
South-west National Park – Tasmania.
It sounded like a last will and testament – the audacity of hope?
'How do you get there?'
You take a light plane from Hobart.
It's only a 7-seater so you feel…everything!
It would have been simpler to read the doc my poem
'Towards Melaleuca'.
And now I know the needle has gone into my arm –
a sliver of irritation.

Looking up into the lights – my eye a sea of jelly
under a double moon.
The perfect sun of thin-air Everest – or Killaman!
Must we meddle with heaven – *who* let us in?
Landscape's gaze is dawning on Gulliver:
'Graves and glory lost do not make a country.'
Am I doomed to quote myself to myself?
in Dog Days getting ready for the next performance
till the cows come home;
the crow-headed man saying, 'take me by the hand.'

Meantime, the doctor and his assistant
are talking about a looming medical conference in the US:
'if we could discuss *that,* you were doing OK!' I was told later.
And deft and unhurried – is the naming and claiming
of each instruction,
instrument and setting adjustment.
I had been the youngest person in the 'casualty ward'.
The induction nurse had helped me tie my smock.
'A legacy of keeping your looks, huh?' the registrar later smirked.

We never did talk our way back from Melaleuca
or those other ice-edge heights…
And now I'm being wheeled into recovery.
More blood pressure graphs and a thermometer in my ear.
There was still no preview of the outcome:
instead a swath of masking tape bound half my face.
I still needed oxygen in the anteroom.
How plausible was it then? – that I would later wake
as the 13-year-old who hadn't needed glasses.
My long-buried 20-20 uncovered
under time's snowy layers.

# MH 017

You've been in the air 4 or 5 hours.
They may be about to – or have just finished – serving a meal.
It's a bright day outside.
You have the blind up.
You are looking into the blue
remembering something.
Revisiting another time and place,
another journey flying somewhere.
Someone close to you who is not with you.
A child keeps making noises somewhere behind.
You watch some people talk and laugh
into the background hum.
A little girl holds your eyes for a moment.

There's a jolt/flash/screech in the brain

And it all stops.
Everything.
Just like that – you don't exist.

'At least this is how it could, mercifully, have happened.'

Malaysian Airlines MH017 was a scheduled passenger flight from Amsterdam to Kuala Lumpur that was shot down over eastern Ukraine on 17 July 2014.

# Loose Tie

for Federico Garcia Lorca – after Ian Gibson

He had a loose-fitting tie
you know the type artists wear.
I noticed it as I saw the bodies lying there.
That and the clean skin of his fingers.
My name is Manuel Castillo Blanco – volunteer gravedigger.

They were bringing them in every day at that time.
The prisoners would be told, 'you'll be sent to do some roadwork.'
But an hour before dawn – just before the car came for them –
the adjutant would quietly say,
'Your time is short. Do you want to take absolution?
The priest is here.'
At first the artist refused but then he changed his mind
just after the priest had left.
The adjutant served as a proxy witness to his halting, final prayers.
Those he had shared with his mother were so long ago.

The winding drive that followed
seemed both temporary but interminable.
The mind makes a mockery of logic in such moments.
Instead wanders to: 'there was no moon last night.
Where are the birds this morning?'
Even when he and the bullfighters, his two companions in that car,
were given one last offer
the artist had no words.
There was just a jerk of the head
before the shot.

I wasn't there obviously – but the guy who did the deed
said it should have been a clean kill
but he had to give the artist the 'big number' to finish it off.
He apparently liked to get it like that – from a lover.

The weeping women would come later to this park –
but the bodies had all been moved.
The grass has grown back fitfully
where we had to rip up the earth again in our haste.
That was disappointing for the Fascists
who wanted to make it seem as though nothing had happened.
But ghosts won't settle on our demand.
The artist's tie was never tightened.
Why do I tell you all this?
Because they'll probably come for us, the necessary witnesses, next.
The volunteers who were told, 'do this or it's over for you too
when we are in power.'

We are one more loose end that will have to be fixed.

## Ghost Bird

It was just – there.
Vaguely signalled at first.
A single voice amplified, a chorus
along the thoroughfares of mind,
a once-loved soul
confirming its immortality perhaps,
an echo – like some kind of sob,
half-way to sleep in another room.
The hairline of wound
behind the bloom of blood,
a warning.
A night-crawler – no shape but sound
miming the loop of our common script.
A conversation in dreams…
At 2 a.m. in August
the ghost bird of spring
is telling you
it's later than you think.

# Carnarvon Gorge

When we turned the corner
from the falling world of branches
our steps down formed an echo
and shadows on the sheer walls
showed red ochre blown against outspread hands
to make a pattern.
It told the legends of this grove.
The softly gathering drops
of mist condensing in the
grey first light
spelt conversations from divining frequencies
that endure in
tongues of bird calls;
lapping at our memory –
a story that lives now in the stone.

Yesterday, today, for all time.

# In Harm's Way

As Mr Cliché, the arbiter of what we do and why, would have it,
'Put yourself in harm's way often enough
And your number will surely come up.'
Even when the details represent the 'worst' luck imaginable.
Steve Irwin's stingray getting a bullseye shot
right into the heart.
Brockie's car hitting a solitary tree, side-on
at just the angle to impact the driver worst!
In situations that no one
no matter how legendary in skills and expertise
could have provided for.
These guys had so many 'like' scrapes over the years
never fooling themselves they could cheat
the Ultimate Outcome if it came.
It's scant justification to friends, hero-worshippers
even family
that they went out there again, thinking,
'I know what I'm doing – the odds, the probability
of it coming unstuck over time.
Just as I know I'd rather be doing this
than anything else.
I have to know those things –
or I've got no business taking up this space.'

# To Ted Hughes

on reading his *Birthday Letters*

The result was as inevitable as your retreat
from all those gossips.
But in an attempt to finally embrace what – tenderness? –
you discovered only domesticity's vile purity.
Poetry, as description, the pathos sans power.
A novel you finally should have written.
Yet in prose so purple/personal,
a confessional movie we would all want to see –
not a *poetry* bestseller!
A jerker where secrets become banal,
gossip has a flow – commentary,
with discipline's tightrope vanished.
Grist unrelenting though
for the mass media psycho-couch mill,
as if to capitulate: 'Oh yes, I *need* this analysing!'
Stripped of cryptics and janus-faced clues,
cowed, like a baby cradled:
'I tell you – this double is my real self, too!'
'I can't be that strong and silent. *Any* more!'
It was the lesson you found, inside
of your failings, before that other, German, Father/rival.
Her landscape's shadow side more chilling
than your Promethean crags, your eagles' eyrie,
the life of Dante on Moortown's farm,
Mytholmroyd – the seat of all visions!
All cudgels to carry, too late now,
to deserted houses where she had been.

Time seems to have twisted about:
in 'gratitude' for your guidance she'd burnt your wings.
Like your words left mine, stillborn, when I got too close,
visions too vivid to merely reiterate,
captured in that queer safety of living in the absolute,
the electricity of the impulse, the 'unnameable'.
As if you really were some emissary from our End:
'I know! The Crow will be the all-hero! Phoenix and entrails, both.'

What you couldn't do for her was reach her.
But they were only words after all, those weapons writ large,
only events with points of view – only the heart can know in itself.
With humility, our frail mortality can be excused those misfires,
as nothing compared to the Awful Blank,
which no universe in an atom can prepare for,
no thought scrawled, can distract from.
That place where she,
having escaped the need of Daddy and false father figure,
motherhood even – the kids never able to budge
the drugged figure from the oven door –

arrived, before you.

# Chet Baker

American jazz soloist on TV in France

Physique of an athlete
rock star looks
the rainbow was inside him!
All he needed to flee with was his blessed horn
and the microphone he made love to.

All the way to Paris
female accomplices flinging themselves
at his baggage.
A reinfusion into the Old World: Europe
'Chic Americain on Boulevard St Germain.'
Smoky bars under the melody's spell
that ivory tinkle – that fat lizard bass
that husk of velvet
that temptress: something extra.

Left with a family of 3 in Oklahoma
his wife says, 'It was always difficult –
as someone outside –
splitting the artist from the man.'

Now the rooms are smaller –
built around a sink, a mattress
an open window on the alley.
The mirror etching the missing teeth.
The face eaten out by cocaine.
The body sterile and emaciate.
Those eyes that would not recognise a square meal.

It's all in the smoke now
the crowded banquettes
the athlete of memory – trying to muster one last impulse
against the clamour of that relentless in-crowd.
By now it could be anyone 'up there'.
Somehow it finds the decency to pause,
listen for the rasp too weak for the horn
a ghost's nudge in a dream:
'I'm almost there. Almost there…almost blue.'

From offstage – in a hurried timbre,
'Lights out. That's a wrap.'

## Zeroes

The tides had prevented the children being moved to land
the previous night. The refugees were being offloaded
from the lighter:
'Looks like an orphanage' someone quipped at the kids' faces
crammed against the window glass.
'But not one I would ever want to be in.'
Then the droning roar rolled towards them,
the planes swung into view.
'Fighters! It must be the Yanks!'
But it was the Japanese bombers – on their death-dealing raids.

The children's would-be rescuer would live
but the scene would never leave his frozen form:
those plumes from the planes' guns
racing across the water
over and over.
And the boats lit up by the 'Splash! Splash!'
of red-yellow fire.

This incident marked a moment when the Second World War came
to the remote pearl port of Broome, WA.

# How That Fellah Othello Got the Rap

It was never just a matter of black over white
nor simply getting it wrong not right
for a Moor in Venice respect was the key
but he neglected his home, his hearth and ladee.
For all the stature he socially made bold
the bed of his love grew unnaturally cold.

(Chorus): Such a man in charge, such a power-oh
but not above the cunning could he stay!
Such a man in charge such a lord-ho
but a base trick brought him affray.

For, cautioned on the stair by his friend Iago,
Othello heard tell of a wench become farrago.
He became convinced his wife had been swiving
when all the time it was only Iago conniving.
'A lady of deceitful tongue no less.'
A dissembler in the mirror who his hands undressed.

(Chorus): Such a man in charge, such a power-oh
but not above the cunning could he stay!
Such a man in charge such a lord-ho
yet a base trick brought him affray.

Bent by a fear he had been made cuckoo
Othello strangled Desdemona as dawning came true.
For all of his fame made a dung of the Prize
he could never evade those eyes of Sighs.
'Destroyed by love' was the only plea he could hold
to the gaze of the Deity on the public scaffold.

(Chorus): Such a man in charge, such a power-oh
but not above the cunning could he stay!
Such a man in charge such a lord-ho.
Yet a simple trick
brought him affray.

A simple trick brought him affray.

# Posterity Got it Wrong

I'd heard all about the legend
and its disclaimer: genius.
The Vivaldi of the horn
splitting the atom in a sax solo.
Teenage parent, wayward husband, vagrant friend,
dead – not in a car crash
but watching TV at the Baroness's.
The computer-mind, before his time,
too fast to live.
Foster-father of a foreign flame: Paris,
his impatience, rage, insomnia
burnt neurons from inside out.
In the end
I turned on the CD player to hear the accelerating serpent of crying,
amphetamine Iago
against the silence.
It sounded like the repeater-rifle horn,
the 'ack-ack' gun of aches,
was down on the street outside,
blowing storms past my shopfront studio;
a fast-forward opera on the neon starway.

Breath snatched away, I ran to the window,
hurried out and down the stairs,
adrenalin: the opium from nowhere
fizzing through my veins.

But no…no
Parker, Charlie or anyone,
was anywhere
to be found.

# It Always Gets Me

When I think I know all about war,
when I am cynical of fresh starts,
when I tire of tales of courage,
when I count the cost in lives,
when I feel there's no more to find –
the trumpeter starts playing 'The Last Post'.

Signal of regret and yet
winding, finding its way –
it frames the light
to minds lost in the black.

It always gets me.

And I must look up
from the crypt of circumstance…
the clouds have lifted.
'The Last Post' – the first eyes
look on my fate afresh.
And so do I.
And so must I.

# Part Three

# In Wake of Adam Cullen

Life is a bowl of cherries
but people distrust the simple.
When it takes too much pain to keep going:
'I don't want to tell anyone anything any more.
Except: endurance is more important than truth.
That's not original.'

He was caught between addiction
and the body's failure before abuse.
The art was almost incidental.
'I love it because it's so useless.
The cat was skinned while the Doors played – that sort of thing.'

Now he'd won the Archibald.
it took a lot of pain to keep that reputation going.
It's like hitting yourself in the mouth to dull an aching tooth.
'I'm depressed but I'm not completely gutless.
The gun there is actually a metaphor.'
In so doing he burnt the bridge
while he was still crossing it.

'You have to sort of sacrifice yourself.
I think that's what love's about – being scared.
I prefer to hug (men).
And anyway – women just can't do it.'

The court case after the police found the fire-arms in his car
proved how paranoid he'd become.
He wanted to meet up with normal people – but it didn't work:
'I can't make art at home (with da). It's too happy for me!'

The bedroom of the mountain shack was littered with stained sheets. Back in the gallery I kept looking at Goya's picture of Saturn devouring his son,

thinking where Adam had taken himself.

# Shop Window Dummies

for Jill Meagher

The dummies in that shop window,
facsimiles of women's bodies,
are the only witnesses to what happened
as we try and re-plot the sequence;
connect the dots on a blank page –
make a pattern that can explain.

Technology offers only 2-dimensional revelation.
The CCTV inside the Bridal Shop
cannot intimate
what made that figure, in the blue hoodie outside, double back,
compelled to approach
the woman unsteady on her feet.
What did they say? How did they act towards each other
as their random fates crossed?

It's like trying to reconcile why a husband in a flat
seven hundred metres away – falls asleep in front of the TV
when he should have been meeting his wife.
Why a colleague's concerned offer of an escort is waved away.
Why a brother three thousand miles off is rung instead
to be consulted on a family grief.

When the woman's mobile is silenced
reality's final fatal pattern
is set –
as if ordained.

We want to replay that CCTV vision
and get a different ending.

Tell ourselves in the predator: don't trust that urge,
your pattern that motivates.
Warn ourselves in his disorientated target:
the jaws of consequence are closing.

We feel more useless than a shop window dummy.

# No Refuge

Thunder looms, lightning stutters,
to be met by blasphemy's earthbound slings and arrows.
My torch flickers defiantly
an infinitesimal anti-aircraft gun;
a blind reaction ready for the raid.
It flashes to ground also
to trap the phosphorescent
eyes of field mice
fleeing towards my feet as shelter –
a new tree
branching out of my sodden jacket-trunk,
arms awhirl,
a voice booming back from the oak
in a new discovery of curses,
like a Coles Storybook cartoon.
A giant fist hallucinated by an eructing, aimless will
striking through the onset of whipping rain
in one incandescent
flame.

# Old Poet

Upon the death of Dorothy Porter

The queer certainty

of reading other people's poems at 2 a.m.,

you wanting to hold

one last hand

against the dark –

but what is that intimation now

coming back

from the ether?

Friends, colleagues – now acquaintances past…

in our arrogance, our insufficiency,

we never got to ask

about that line, that word

that phrase you used

that simply answered

a question in my head.

Reading poems at 2 a.m.…

no one knowing who they touched.

# From Arles, Provence

Vincent Van Gogh was pursuing his fifth career choice when he decided to travel south from Paris in 1888. So far he had tried, and failed, to be a book salesman, a private tutor, a lay preacher and an art teacher. He was now determined to be an artist – a painter of renown. Fired by his enthusiasm for the modernist perspectives of Japanese prints and painting in the open air, Vincent wanted to emulate the exploits of his great mentor, Jean François Millet. He planned to become such a force other artists would come to Arles to join him in a new art movement.

Paul Gauguin eventually joined Vincent in Arles and the two lived and worked together for some weeks. On the 23rd of December, however, they had a huge row. Gauguin stormed out of the Yellow House in the Place Martine where they lived. Van Gogh ran after him and aggressively confronted him with an open razor. Gauguin then fled towards the town centre. In a highly disturbed state Vincent returned to the Yellow House and cut off most of his left ear. He then walked to a nearby brothel and presented the severed morsel of flesh in a package to a young woman, Gabrielle Berlata, who worked there.

The poems in the following section are an attempt to write Vincent's thoughts around the most famous paintings he executed in Arles – and his brief life there.

## The Second Chair – Bedroom in Arles

I see people go out of this room
as I am about to step into it.
Are they hiding from my need of society?
Returning exhausted from the sunflower fields,
my studies of the clouds and the birds,
I fancy, too, I hear voices.
Are they from my childhood?
Or my still childish ambitions?
On the bed I lie, hearing the clucking of cuckolds;
looking from the cloud shapes to the tangerine ceiling,
the ruby flower design tracing the empty mirror.
The bird calls make chalk marks…
That knock on the door must be the maid.
After so many days' inattention to my appetites
does she secretly want me to hear her confession?
There's only one reason for a second chair in this room.
The 'knock knocks' are like footfalls on the stair
slowly moving…out of reach.

## A Well-lit Café – Café Terrace at Night

I appreciate its stagey demeanour:
the gaslit gold of the awning so perfect
against the star-splotched velvet.
Romance's deep song resting among the advantaged:
the harmony of this Provençal night!
This view is my nourishment
the source of my hunger appeased –
to see those tables so discrete in their aloneness,
to feel the forms moving arm in arm along the street,
mannequins in a stage show
waiting for the dance of commerce to entwine and begin.
The aroma of a feast of dishes now, offstage, lingers.
The waiter is like a priest
attending the pharaohs of industry.
The forms of couples touch, almost reverently
resolving their *pas de deux*,
walking back under the accepting veil of light.
The harmonium whimpers…

## River Rhône Roaming – Starry Starry Night

Stars remind us of our place.
Water transports us across the land.
To feel the muscles of a river
is like watching the stars wheel around the sky,
showing unexpected forces
we cannot influence – but go into the night in sleep
to be transported to other planets
until we come to the place we finally lie.
Looking at the stars makes me dream.
As simply as I dream over the black dots
on a map representing towns and villages.
Why, I ask myself, shouldn't the shiny dots in the sky
be as accessible as those black dots on the map of France?
Just as we take the train to get to Tarascon or to Rouen
we take death to reach that final star.

## The Farming Art – Harvest Landscape

I looked again at the sketch I made last night,
the man and woman gleaners curled into
their warmth on the straw – and felt sleepy.
What did I think I was doing here?
I had walked beyond the hay cart's wide compass
and the gruff brows of the unsuspecting farmer.
I listened to the starlings and wood doves playing
concerto notes among the fences and the stacks.
I should have been sketching the wind-ruffled grasses
and huge, nodding sunflowers
but the far roar of the black bulls stirred me.
My rope throwing itself out to trap
the proud necks of the white horses
like a Camargue cowboy.
This also was in my dream…

## Blackbird Echo – Crows in a Cornfield

Painting can take away every other appetite;
a process of being mentally crushed,
physically drained.
Existence can come down to one or two elements
reiterated over and over in a trance, inside –
while you drink innumerable cups of coffee and wine.
You break more bread you have got on credit,
your pipe filled over and over – and, by smoke, consumed.
You think the picture can come to you
on demand, through endless beginnings and dead ends
no matter what drug it may take.
Outside, the corn field stretches ever ahead.
You wade into it as though entering a wave.
It lures, coiling around your legs and arms.
Your breath fails you
drawn on by a carolling in your head
and a sky jarring, broken by that melody;
clouds black,
with the repeating gale of wings.

## Hope in a Visitor – The Red Vineyard

Gaugin was puzzled by how I chose my colour palette.
How I took my chances with thickly applied paint.
He hated that lack of order.
I painted what I saw, in the main,
whereas Gaugin painted from his imagination.
I completed a picture of my mother when young.
Gaugin encouraged me to make sketches in the brothels.
At our house Gaugin took care of the cooking
and our joint finances.
I saw how good he could be for the Yellow House
and longed for him to get back to the Gaugin of old
with his island girls – and his negresses.
Gaugin said my sunflowers
'Were better than Monet's lilies as Impressionist works.'
After a long walk with Gaugin
I painted the red vineyard – and, in the studio,
two portraits of the café owner
and then a start for the Sower –the canvases just flowed!
Such intelligent company is good for my continuity!
We did not ask ourselves, what can we learn from each other?
But he confessed, 'I feel my old self coming back.'
Though at the end of a day we were both competitive –
there is a wariness.
And, inevitably, this place takes some getting used to.
We feel like – pioneers, really, each time we make a mark.

*The red vineyard* was the only painting sold in Van Gogh's lifetime.

## Bandaged Life – Self-portrait with Bandaged Ear

'I don't know this man. I don't know who he is.
I cannot remember who I am!'
That's what I was told I said to the policeman at the time.
After the first few days in the hospital
I feel myself coming out of my artist's 'fit'.
And the New Year is just around the corner.
The local clergyman came to see me
and reflected on my good spirits.
'I am at work again' I wrote to my mother and my sister,
'and everything is normal.
'I am sorry to have caused Theo such trouble for such a trifle.
'I have made a self portrait: 'with bandaged ear and pipe'
and 'I am sleeping well.'
Meantime, the porter told me the cleaning lady had gone
to the police about my coming back to the Yellow House.
The second time I was discharged I was woken by people
clamouring at my window, and children trying
to climb up on the roof to get a better look.
I was some strange animal in a zoo!
I yelled out! I chased the children off,
I touched the women to make them go away.
They came for me, the police and the mayor's counsel.
I could not go back to my old surroundings –
my landlord had given me notice.
At the end of the month I said to the doctor
I would like to go to the asylum at Saint Remy.

I painted outside in the garden there and the spring grass
was a deep electric green, the lights of blossoms set fire
to the tree branches, the pink-purple trunks twist and dance
like birds about to take off with their jewels, above the
wet-red roofs and the mauve church tower. Very fauve!
One part of me says, 'You are absent-minded and that
surrounds your every turn without help.'
The other says, 'You should have defended your studio
and your dream for the Yellow House to the death.'

## Iris at San Remy – Iris

What possessed me?
What made me walk in that direction
in this garden?
What drew me on beyond my memory?
Beyond the sadness of a lost loved one
or an argument with a relative,
beyond my stillness…
What made me wonder instead
how the garden offers up such gifts.
How nature in her multifarious ways
works out a solution – in such dazzling beauty
such as a man can only dream of making?
What made me stop and look at the iris?
This iris. How I found myself breathing more calmly
the more I gazed upon it.

## The Path Knows the Way – Garden of the Asylum

I have, I think, a predisposition for order,
like these garden beds, their regimentation of colour.
A place for each individual and a variety all included.
And the grounds here, the walk in the garden
of green, and by the pond where the birds gather –
how could they *not* be designed for a similar grace and function?
It's true. I think now about my practice
more than I present it in action.
I compose my pictures in my head alone more often.
Like I accept I should not now so often miss mealtimes
or forget to put on a coat in anticipation of the chill arriving.
I must, I believe, cosset my 'acute mania with general delirium,
and irregularly recurring epileptic attacks' in this way
(with devilish chuckle!)
But just this evening I delayed returning to
those rooms lit by lanterns – finding, in my subterfuge,
the place where there is an opening beyond the glades
I had not noticed before – which I shall investigate.
When next the starry night above directs me.

## The Sower, The Reaper – Sower with the Setting Sun

The orb hangs like a giant orange subduing the landscape.
You could reach up to it
if you weren't drawn to the human depicted here.
His blackened form may betray wishes of trespass;
forbidden tastes. The looming tree;
could be making a noose for failed fruit.
The orb is crowning the Sower
whatever *we* may finally make of him.

# AMSL

At 4,900 metres we came across a flapping sound.
Lights over dark forms on the farthest campsite. My hands felt cold.
I asked Steve at the next halt, 'Have you gone to full glove yet?'
'Hell, yeah, Hollywood!'
I could feel where sweat had frozen in my balaclava.
At 5,000 metres it was snowing again.
You could see it being driven against your face as you
were side-on to your companion's beam.
The push ahead became tunnel vision – sightless exertion.
The path slippery and indistinct.
Every time we stopped it took eight or so big deep breaths
to regain equilibrium.
At 5,200 metres the snowfall was gone – the wind dropped.
Glasses fogged. There's an interminable time drying them
with the left glove off.
Now you see it – the red line on the horizon behind you –
the unknown being outstretched.
Mantle of day. Then someone says,
'Danny – your head torch is still on!'
5,500 metres AMSL. More people around in the distance.
We are operating on fumes.
Any capitulation would be very public for the pride.
You say to Charles, 'It looks like three more pushes up' –
realise it's probably five.
The final exertion as we thought was only to Stella Point –
5,700 metres.
At 5,895 the guide turns to embrace you.
'God bless you, Charles,' you eruct, not realising that it's Samuel.
Charles is down there somewhere with Peter or Mike.
One question: AMSL – what the devil does it mean?

'Above mean sea level,' Samuel laughs, pouring tea from his thermos.
Above means so little!
The summit is called Uhuru.
And there's the wooden sign to prove it.
Only you can reconcile this Gingerbread Land to yourself
as your companions arrive.
The air of heaven has a fluffy, edible feel to it.

# Tarangere, Tanzania

Here that water-scrooge, the baobab, dominates.
It is the last month of the scheduled dry season.
The creek beds are exhausted, the grass almost white.
In the middle of the day baboon, monkey and eland, hide.
Antelope groups cluster then separate.
Wildebeest trail off in their migrations to the rains, north,
then come back, betraying their clan.
Hippos are curvy mounds – more and more exposed
from the mud to cool them.
The giraffes move like ghosts in a chess-dance with thirst,
diprotodon heads half-raised: swaying, probing.
Life here until the cloud fall will get increasingly uncomfortable.
Seeking a short cut, our jeep is suddenly trapped
on the river's cracked-boulder border.
As we get out to push we are standing
in the huge pads of the last dinosaur's footmarks,
brains ajelly with the expectation,
shake of earth at his footfall.

# Grasping the Bacon

Francis in Australia

In the studio the PR adage comes to me:
'You think chaos – he thinks order.'
But a magnetism is shared:
the bare bones, the decapitated head – of Our Cruxifiction.
And…burn victims – possibly napalm.
What's the attraction?
The energy of protoplasm
in an artificial environment
signalled by body fluid smudges.

'What of it, cobber?
Flickerty and Flackerty we are.'

Muybridge's running dog
is but a pulse, a flimsy ribbon…
Think animals on post rails; a meat rack.
Drug addicts and body builders,
wrestlers grappling or copulating – take your pick.
Homosexuals trapped in screams
and business suits
ape popes of a hidden faith.
A deviants' ballet beyond bars…

'What of it, cobber?
You look like you like it rough!
Flickerty and Flackerty we are.'

Does he really see Isobel and his other friends that ugly way?
Facial movements' time lapse
superimposed in portrait.
Flesh under radiation
somehow strikes a chord;
beauty beyond our recoil
setting modern nerves ajar.
Risky, accidental, outsiderist poster boy?
Or eccentria's Furniture Designer
become outrage-kitsch?

'What of it, cobber?
Beg my harsh rules to soften?
Pig's beer, my dear!
But look, this one of the doctor is almost gentle, yeah?

I am starting to see an order here –
Flickerty and Flackerty – in triptych
on the next to last morning (of the world)…
in my mirror
– half a man shaving.

# What Happened Last Night?

A reflection on David Hockney's *Portrait of an Artist,* 1972

I am staring down at the body
trying to make sense of…
I am thinking – in this beautiful, isolated landscape
in the driest state in the Union
we try to paint the way the light reflects
through these several strata of water –
and that's the most important thing.
But I'm frowning down at the body
and thinking, it's a gated estate community out here
miles from any police.
If I don't report this – will anyone ever know?
It's been a cynical ride I know.
All media works like this now.
We've exploded the myth of the god-holy consumption being positive
and let reign about all the other contradictions and hypocrises
as though the Vietnam war, et cetera – or the struggle for us boys
would ever impinge on Home Beautiful.
We fancy 'outrageous' is our middle name.
The cat is out of the bag
but we still shrink from the claw marks.

Now I'm back at my desk staring at the phone.
Trying to see the future
put something behind me.
I can already see myself loving again…
Making that light play and refract
in shadows over that inert form…
We had an argument last night
and Peter ran off.
I blotted myself out until dawn.
I'm trying to blot out that inert form
as I stare into the water again.
Peter, the athletic goat,
would frighten the hell out of me sometimes by playing 'dead'
after a couple of laps.

What happened last night?

The death of pop.

## Inalarga Pass

It was as if the body, the skin, absorbed that land's message
through the senses –
and the response was registered in a trance – unable now,
to be recalled exactly.
A blessing, a poem I uttered to the landscape.
I read it out as it came to mind – 'pure' and 'untramelled'
like a verbal to the heavens.
I wish I could remember the best parts.
This pass is a bridge between two peoples
different Aboriginal custodians – the Arrente and the Luritja.
If you are a member of tribe A you have to get permission
or be accompanied by a member of tribe B
whose territory you are entering.
My words were thanking the Creator of this bridge between tribes
attesting to the healing power of this land
even after so many abuses have been committed;
its rough beauty, its flesh of stone, life-giving colours and tree-song
its sun in nature's coldest season.
There was a sadness too which lent weight to the process.
I could not seriously attempt the next section of this trail
because of my injuries, faults in my application, failure of my quest
to realise my completion.
Unlike the two tribes whose land this was.

Someday I will recall the best parts of my prayer.

# Drought and Beyond

In this the book of the Land – and the lives of its servants:
'My brother took on this farm with an eye for profit.
But 16 years later break-even hasn't begun!'
Suicide in honour raises one family's last flag of occupation
in boom, bust, hope and renewal.
Look at this starving sheep – more shadow than flesh
in this aridity most heartless – and its master *still* seeks to save it!
A dead horse dragged by tractor to the knackery
one sightless eye like a button sewed onto a face.
Others, the low-light moon-cattle, are herded gently – no
curses, no whip-cracking
and the meat will be all the more tender that way.
A lone sheep is pulled from the mud – part of its face hacked away
in a heartbeat for a crow-beak
feeding like the vulture on Prometheus' liver.
The widening furrow of a horse's ribcage echoed
by mangle in its owner's face.
There is also the crucially comic at a lake of dust resort
a posted boat sign – speed limit: five knots;
a high-diving ramp surveys frozen bed of stricken earth.
There are the bushfire scenes: at King Lake,
'five minutes after we got out we'd have been toast!'
The horror etched indelibly in the eyes, the slackness of jaw:
'This – a dustbowl – this was my future!'
A wracked paddock addressed by 'For Sale – Ray White, S.E.'
Yet this book of earth has to end with hope.
A single shower, brief in its halo touch, on a farm
in Midlands, Tasmania
has a kelpie looking at its owner with almost a gleam.

A family on return to a WA wheat farm:
having seen the worst now prays the best would take
its turn around them next.
Vibrant parents and kids – what else makes any sense?
As we in the city tut-tut: 'the price of this fruit and veg
is so high this week!'
Ravaged faces, dust smites, tractor whirls – a man leans
against a couple of bales he can still hope to sell.
Another man on a mobile phone surveys an emaciated harvest
now hit by frost *and* drought compounding: 'who's he gunna call?'
Another figure with his young son crumb soil between their fingers.
The father has never seen the riverbed so clearly.
The child has never seen the rain that could change it.
'Beyond reasonable drought…'
Sometimes survival *is* the pot of gold for decades' dedication.

# Moses at Finke

It gives the Larapinta its name.
Sand river – flowing into the desert – not towards the sea.
Could Moses have been found
in the rushes that now sprout
above the green-blue water?
Could the Aboriginal's religious source
actually be the *father* of all other such disciplines?
Disseminated from the sand tower of some Babel now eroded.
Where the spirit first stood up in man
stars are so close to the ground at 6 a.m.
so different from the winking ice crystals of the night before.
The Glen Helen waterhole/gorge
long before it fed cattle, was a drought refuge.
The Finke the centre of trade links and songlines;
witness to the passage of pearl shells
from the Kimberley and Broome;
red ochre from the Flinders Ranges –
an economic chain that linked all tribes.
Before whitemen later ran stock on the floodplains
in the hills surrounding this place – Itye the Moon Man
took his mistress to be his love,
their guilty laughter frozen
into the winds that called her name;
while their children nosed through the glitter
and the water shadows; in bony bream, spangled and
black-striped grunter – Macdonnell Ranges rainbow.
And a man in a robe with a storm of beard
the morning after – knelt to drink.

# Birthnight

The midges had almost gone when something nudged me – some faint breeze…anyway, I came up for air. I was gazing at the panoply of stars and the Southern Cross – by the tree branches right over my head. Here was the full regalia! Of castor sugar and salt flung against the velvet – and I just drank it in for long moments. With the sound of mopoke owls and the something seeking repetition of tawny frogmouths, over and over. The odd bird or mouse squeak. This was outback nocturnal spate again with all the trimmings. The feint hush of wind and the sky moving to the left, the stars moving I'd watched them so long. And when I finally turned to lie on my side – there was the moon. Just a single steady light growing, birthing into sight through branch brackets, the surrounding sky spread wide for her wonder.
About four hours later I saw the day's sun born into the same space. As if arriving upon a dark vault just crystalising from its coldest hour,
the half-bashful, half-daring peeps of finches fidgeting in the foliage beside my tent.
I will later hear the hundredth different bird call carving its path across the blue.
The trees' shadows changing position against the sun – I'd watched them so long.

# Time Belongim You, Massa

When I opened my eyes again
couldn't see ahead or behind,
looked at my watch – no match for the others' sixth sense
on this mountain – like my laced boots
versus the sandshoe bravado of native boys.
How long will the mist hold me in its grasp?
Then a stone whistled past my ear and I ducked.

Back at the halfway lodge I felt small, cheated,
the Seventh Day Adventist boys having seen the summit
and the sun setting.
'We did it for Sammy, boss,' said Kemsun
stirring the rice and shaving the boiled yam.
Humbled, I smiled at last: 'Is he coming back to Goroka with you?'
'He has to go home to his village. He has payback to settle.
That's why Fat Boy Rasta is here.'
Fat Boy had just rejoined us, superior, all-knowing.
I looked into his eyes. He'd thrown that stone at me, I knew.
'Like us, Sammy wanted to see where God lives first,' Joey added.

Next day the boys went down ahead of me.
Having 'survived' Mount Wilhelm they were proud –
incognisant of my tread again into some sleeping dread.

# Visiting Santa

Today, I went to see Santa at his village
near Rovalinen in Finland; known folksily as Santa's Birthplace.
Here it is Christmas every day.
Sleigh camps and reindeer and husky workshops
dot the Arctic Circle forests all around.
I had a two minute interview and a photo
taken with the Master.
Before that I wondered at all the things people tell him
whether I should talk about my childhood, Xmases past.
Like God there must be all the arguments he would have to settle
on the spot – from the faithful and the villain, equally.
How he had to be humble and understand, while crazies ranted.
It must be easier for him if you had a child with you.
Would he even speak English?
Would he look, ineluctably, Finnish?
I seemed to be waiting a long time for our audience.
I'd forgotten the dazzling array of items in the gift shop
I'd had to pass through to get to that modest room.
Frantically, I began to forget all the issues I felt I should raise.
I remembered my wife's wishes (she is a vegan)
that he should make sure the reindeer so important to him
always get enough to eat and drink, and be kept
as warm and dry as possible…
Eventually *that* became the only thing important I should say to him.
And suddenly I was seated beside him, resplendent and white-bearded
in his Santa suit. He greeted me with a burr-like 'hello'.

When I came back out to the street in that little town
I felt I'd done my duty. I didn't need the photo souvenir
of him and me.
The receptionist looked disappointed behind her smile.
But that was only temporary, even theatrical, I knew.
There is *always* another customer
in this place many would think of as heaven.

# 'All That is Left'

A woman reflects on Auschwitz

'What is great in Man is that he is a bridge and not a goal; what is loveable about Man is that he is a transition and a downfall.'
– Friedrich Nietzsche, from *Thus spake Zarathustra*

(i)

There was loud music playing in the adjutant's office.
You could still hear the people coughing on the gas in the showers
and children crying. Later, the smell of human flesh burnt in the ovens.
The gold in their teeth had been salvaged of course.

(ii)

It's not what's outside that's most vital.
I am not living in the past.
The past however is alive in me.
I hold this object as a reminder
of what, who I was, then.
What my loved ones later held.
What their hands touched with such love.

(iii)

It is the one thing I had when it was all over
to put in this ceremonial display now.
A blanket made from human hair
gathered from concentration camp in-mates
who'd been shorn before their shower.
Why was it gathered and reused – and who did that?

(iv)

The Hungarian, the collaborator with the Nazis,
flung the blanket away as she was exposed –
for a survivor, me, to warm herself with

I was 29 kilos and starving then.

# Flame-lighter

I don't really like groups.
I join them sometimes
when we drive out, on patrol
with all our gear – like an army…
Old days.
But they don't need me.
I want to move towards the flame
to quietly absorb its dance
its colours and movement.

I've walked this bush so many times
it's like a second skin.
When the hot air seems to thicken with a hum, a roar
could that just be my blood and heart racing?

A sigh-hymn in the wind
the branches' arms – moving, beckoning …
it's not something I could talk to anyone about
that private show only I can feel, can make again.

The roar seems all inside me now
as I watch the flame catching hold.
I close my eyes
feeling like always
a soothing in my head's din.
This comfort, this making sense…

but I cannot help but watch.

# State of Disunion

The planet is burning.
There is no government.
There are only market penetrations.
There is only capital society cannot access.
There is only control,
shareholders from 'other where', hide.
They teat-feed those entitled vultures
that we call a parliament.
They overcharge for heat, for cold, for locomotion.
They bastardise our food supplies.
They hostage and quarantine our resources
and meantime, invaders frack-up the tree-cleared farms,
poison our aquifers before the 1,000-skull flood
or dead-fish tide in the Murray Darling.
'This is Me' media force-feed our distractions
and plot our actions and thoughts for manipulation.
They, too, are beyond regulation.
Child abusers run the churches
while right-wing freebooters fire on the praying forms of their enemies.

The planet is burning.
There is no government.
There are only shrinking future projections.
We seek a picture of the latest extinct species
wondering if any care for anyone is valued –
till we see the eyes of our children
in the flames.

# Watching Men Moon Walk

Go with the symbolism we are urged.
Trust the legend not the story.
But is this grainy flicker in fitful light
really us in other worlds' sight?
On the ground our lofty ambitions
and gifted bouquet of goodwill, are stripped,
as rock and foundation corrode and erode.
The newspaper that wrapped the Last Fish,
the dying flower,
our entitled legacy, our science of lost species
and forgotten raindrops – the miracle of colours
in layered memory comfort –
are dusty to the breath.

# Zoo Motions

Taronga Park

The little penguins are so swift
they could be flying through the water.
One by one the rainforest birds
are scared up to meet their netted sky –
like some half-ache we keep remembering.
The male lion's mane made him so much larger than his mate
but there was royalty in their shared power.
As the silver-back approached the glass partition
he was a celebrity compressing an explosion.
While flash cameras and home-movie modules whirred
he suddenly presented his posterior:
'and frankly, ladies and gents, you can kiss my arse!'
Now tigers are on the move,
bumping, bouncing, coil-spined,
up and off the smell of 'lunch'.
You ran with them; their barred interplay
striping back and forth.
Beastly action's proximity
froze kids at this dream become life.
Spectators formed a brotherhood
that was rejected by this Outsider –
his society-minotaur leer in the rear-view mirror
predating on his fellows' grateful expressions.
He studied, almost enviously, the crocodile's inert trunk.

A bark afloat, claws flayed and empty,
you might pass off as dead
on the way to the waterhole…
where a child-boy danced near,
heedless in sing-song cries;
unaware either of vagrant urges that spring.
Beasts in the night
at safari hour in suburban lounge rooms.

www.ingramcontent.com/pod-product-compliance
Lightning Source LLC
Chambersburg PA
CBHW070908080526
44589CB00013B/1223